WHAT DOES A BAROMETER DO?

WHAT DOES A

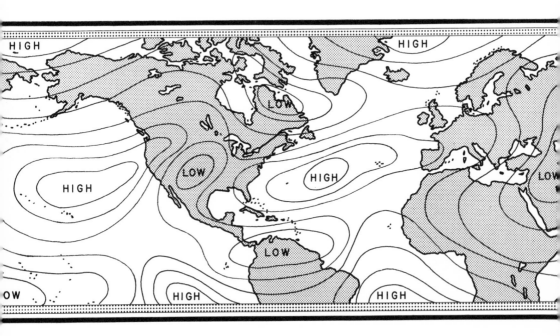

pictures by Len Darwin

BAROMETER DO ?

by William Courtney

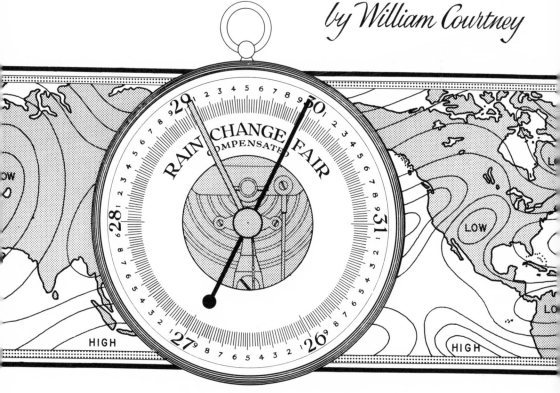

An Atlantic Monthly Press Book
LITTLE, BROWN AND COMPANY
BOSTON   TORONTO

ATLANTIC–LITTLE, BROWN BOOKS
ARE PUBLISHED BY
LITTLE, BROWN AND COMPANY
IN ASSOCIATION WITH
THE ATLANTIC MONTHLY PRESS

Published simultaneously in Canada
by Little, Brown & Company (Canada) Limited

PRINTED IN THE UNITED STATES OF AMERICA

What Does a Barometer Do?

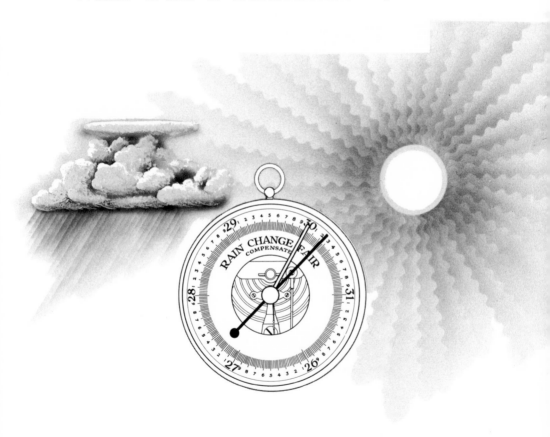

A barometer is one of the most important tools a weatherman uses. It helps tell what tomorrow's weather will be.

Weathermen use barometers because they must tell people ahead of time what the weather will be: bright and sunny or cloudy and rainy.

Sailors use barometers too. They use them to learn if there is a storm ahead. Farmers use them to learn if it is going to rain.

How can a barometer tell us what the weather will be? It tells us by measuring the weight of air pushing against the earth.

And air does have weight. People may say something is "light as air"—but air isn't light at all! It weighs a lot. It is piled up over all the oceans and all the land in the world. It covers the earth like a thick, heavy blanket.

Air is made up of molecules. Molecules are made of two or more atoms—the smallest bits of matter found in Nature. Air molecules are too small to be seen by even the most powerful microscope in the world.

There are many more air molecules in the world than there are grains of sand on all the beaches of the world. Air molecules cover the earth, making a blanket hundreds of miles thick. This blanket is called the atmosphere.

Most molecules that form air are either oxygen molecules or nitrogen molecules.

Each one of the air molecules weighs a little bit—so little you would never notice it. But millions and millions of air molecules weigh a lot. If you could catch all the air molecules in an average-sized bedroom and weigh them, they would weigh nearly seventy-seven pounds.

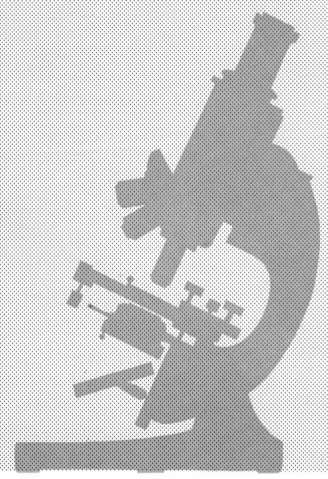

AIR ENOUGH TO COVER THE POINT OF A
PIN WOULD CONTAIN MORE MOLECULES
THAN THERE ARE DOTS ON THIS PAGE.

But air molecules are always moving around. They move up and down, and sideways, and back and forth. They move in every direction.

They push on everything they touch. They push on each other, too, when they meet.

Air molecules near the earth are pushed down by the weight of all the molecules on top of them. A barometer measures how hard these molecules press on the earth. It measures the atmospheric pressure—how hard the atmosphere presses on the earth.

6

The air pressing down on your desk top at school pushes with more force than the weight of your family car! On a piece of wood the size of your desk top, air molecules press down with a force of more than five thousand pounds. That's two-and-a-half tons!

Why doesn't your desk cave in? Because air presses in all directions: up, down and sideways. So the air *underneath* your desk presses *up* with a force of two-and-a-half tons, too. The push *down* is the same as the push *up;* it comes out even—and your desk doesn't even bend.

Air pushes on you, too. When you hold out your hand, air pushes down on it with a force of nearly a hundred pounds. But you don't feel it. The air underneath your hand pushes up with a force of a hundred pounds and exactly balances the push from above.

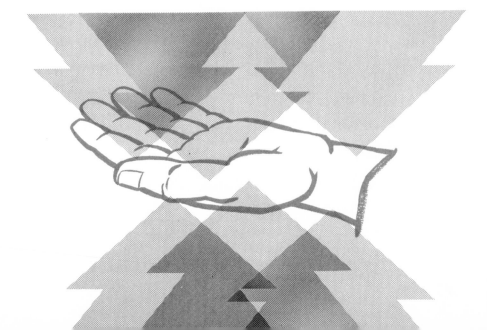

Weathermen discovered long ago that air pushes harder on some days than on others. When air pushes very hard, the weather usually is good. When air doesn't push very hard clouds come. Rain or snow often comes, too, and sometimes there are dangerous storms.

By watching a barometer weathermen know how hard the air is pushing.

But exactly *how* does a barometer tell when the air is pushing hard or not so hard?

To answer this we have to know how a barometer is built. The first one was built a long time ago by a man named Evangelista Torricelli. He was an Italian scientist. Here is how he invented it.

He took a long, thin glass tube like a giant soda straw and closed off one end. Then he filled the tube with a heavy liquid metal called mercury.

Next he poured more mercury into a bowl.

He put his thumb over the open end of the filled tube, and turned it upside down. He pushed his thumb and the end of the tube beneath the surface of the mercury in the bowl. Then he took his thumb away from the end of the tube. He was holding the tube upside down in the bowl of mercury, but the mercury didn't run out. It stayed up in the tube!

Torricelli believed he knew why the mercury stayed up. He had guessed that the air would press down hard enough on the mercury in the bowl to hold the mercury up in the tube. And it did.

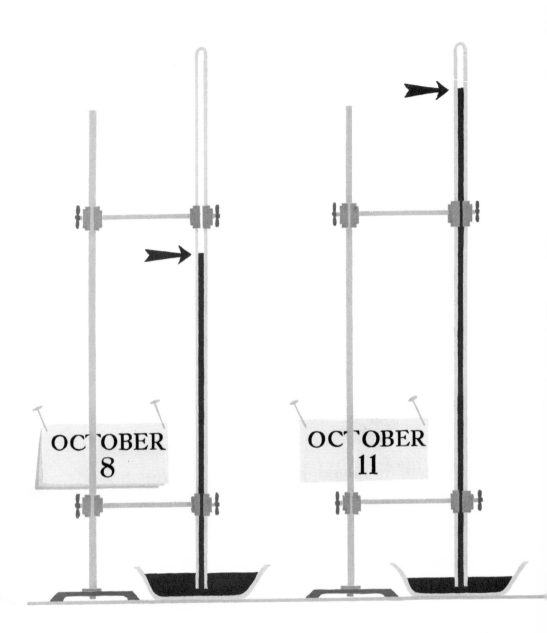

THE HEIGHT OF THE MERCURY CAN VARY FROM DAY TO DAY.

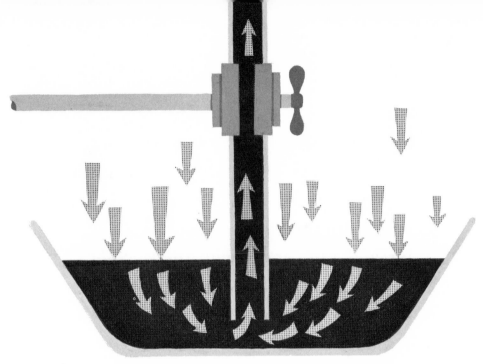

He fastened the tube to a stand so he wouldn't have to hold it, and watched the mercury in the tube as the days passed.

On some days the mercury sank in the tube. On other days it climbed.

Heavy air, pushing hard on the mercury in the bowl, shoved it far up in the tube. When the air was light, it didn't push so hard and some of the mercury ran from the tube down into the bowl.

You can test Torricelli's barometer idea with a simple experiment.

Fill a dishpan or bathtub with water. Take a drinking glass and put it underneath the water. Move it until all the air bubbles out of it. Then turn the glass upside down under the water and raise it, slowly, till the bottom is above the surface. Be careful not to let the rim of the glass come above the surface. See how the water stays up in the glass?

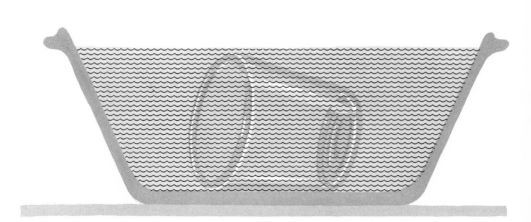

What keeps it up there?

Air pressure keeps it up; air pressing on the surface of the water in the tub. Air pressure is the weight of air on each square inch of surface.

If you had a glass tube long enough you could make a water barometer like Torricelli's

mercury barometer. But you would have to have a tube thirty-four feet long, as tall as a two-story house!

Torricelli used mercury so he wouldn't have to use such a long tube. Mercury is almost fourteen times as heavy as water. This means that one bucket of mercury weighs as much as fourteen buckets of water. So you don't need as much mercury as you do water to balance the air pressure. That's why Torricelli used it. With mercury he needed a glass tube only about thirty-four inches long instead of thirty-four feet.

To tell what the air pressure is at any one time, weathermen measure the height of the mercury in the tube. Usually they measure it in inches. When they talk of such a measurement they mean that the air pressure is enough to hold up a column of liquid mercury just so many inches high.

Average air pressure holds up nearly thirty inches of mercury.

High pressure holds up more than thirty inches of mercury.

Low pressure holds up less than thirty inches of mercury.

For many years scientists used mercury barometers. They placed the bowl of mercury and the tube filled with it in a safe place where it wouldn't be spilled. But if someone did spill the mercury, the barometer had to be filled again. Also, it was hard to move a mercury barometer. Every time someone moved one, there was a chance of spilling the mercury—and mercury costs a lot, nearly ten dollars a pound. It also weighs a lot. A pint jar filled with mercury weighs almost fourteen pounds.

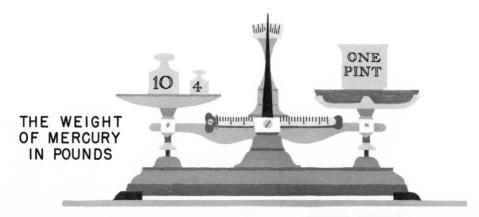

THE WEIGHT
OF MERCURY
IN POUNDS

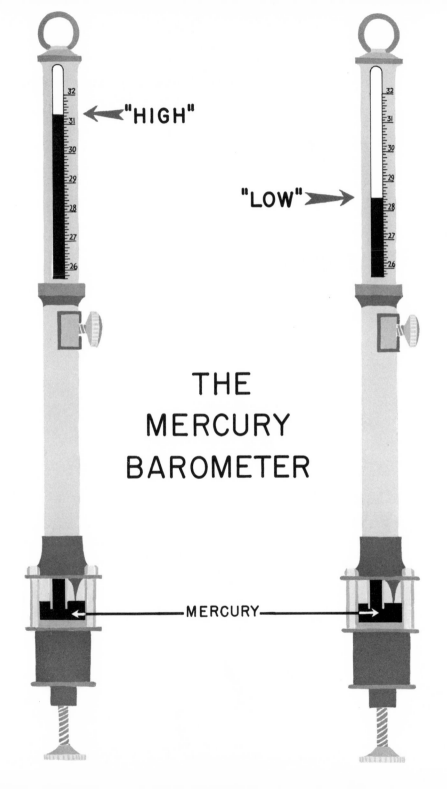

"HIGH"

"LOW"

THE
MERCURY
BAROMETER

MERCURY

So another kind of barometer was invented. It is called the "aneroid" barometer. "Aneroid" means "without liquid."

Aneroid barometers are more complicated than mercury barometers, but they are handy to hang on a wall. They can be moved easily, because there is no mercury to spill. And they are cheaper.

Aneroid barometers are round and have a glass cover. They look something like a wall clock, or a speedometer. Behind the glass is a curved piece of metal called a dial. The dial is marked in inches, the same measurement that the mercury barometer has. Even though there is no mercury in an aneroid barometer, its markings show how many inches of mercury the air could hold up.

The lowest mark on most dials is twenty-eight inches. The highest is about thirty-two inches. Air pressure almost never goes below twenty-eight inches or above thirty-two inches.

In front of the dial are two hands like those on a clock. One of the hands is moved by the weather. You can move the other one with a little knob on the front of the glass. Each time you look at the barometer, you set the movable hand right on top of the other hand. Then the next time you look at the barometer, you can tell which way the weather moved its hand— and how far.

The hand the weather moves may move very slowly. It may move only a little part of an inch during a whole day. Or for several days it may hardly move at all.

How does air pressure make this hand move?

Of course it doesn't push the hand back and forth. It pushes on a small, flat tin can near

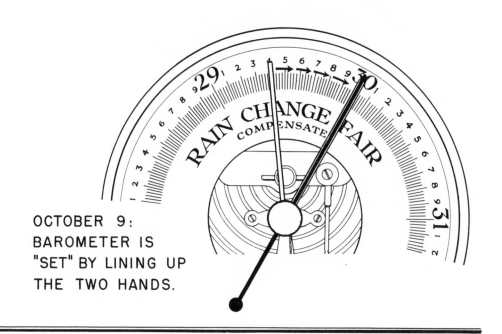

OCTOBER 9:
BAROMETER IS
"SET" BY LINING UP
THE TWO HANDS.

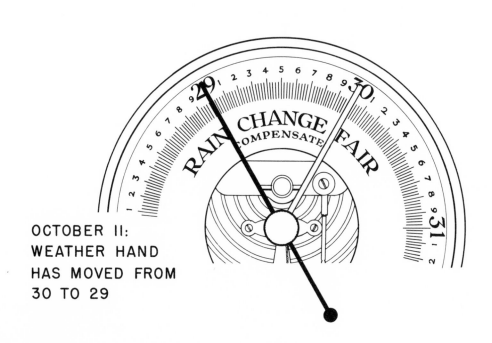

OCTOBER II:
WEATHER HAND
HAS MOVED FROM
30 TO 29

WITHOUT WEIGHT OF AIR

NO
AIR
OUTSIDE

NO AIR INSIDE

AIR PRESSURE ON THE CAN

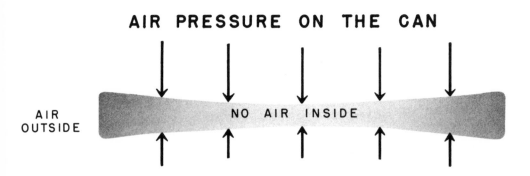

AIR
OUTSIDE

NO AIR INSIDE

the back of the barometer. This small tin can has most of the air taken out of it.

Air pushes against the empty can and bends it in. As the air pressure changes, the bending changes too.

24

You can see how this happens by pressing your hand against an empty gallon can that has flat sides. When you press in the middle of the sides, the metal bends in. When you take your hand away, the metal straightens out again. Air pressure does this on the small can in an aneroid barometer.

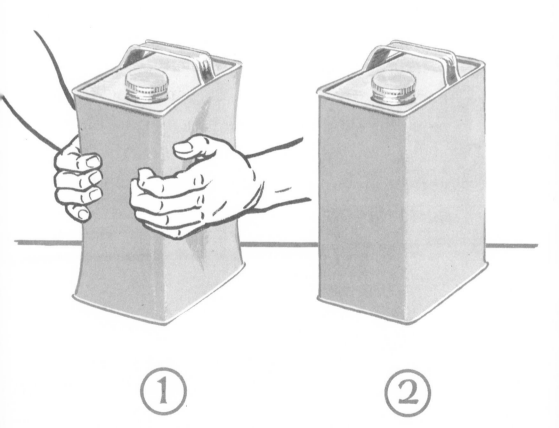

①   ②

In some barometers a small closed tube of thin metal is used instead of a can. But the can or tube is so small, and the bending is so small, that you would never notice it. To make the little bending big enough to see, some way has to be found to make the little motion move something a lot more.

One of the ways this is done is by using a lever. You can see how a lever works by using a pencil and your fingers. Take a pencil and hold it near one end with your thumb and one finger. With one finger of your other hand move the short end of the pencil up and down a little bit. As you do this, watch the other end. It moves a lot more than the short end, doesn't it?

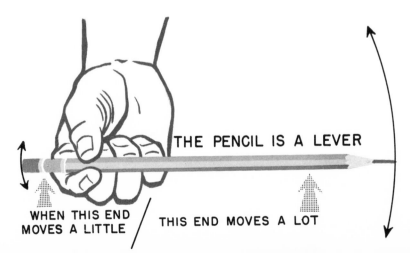

THE PENCIL IS A LEVER

WHEN THIS END MOVES A LITTLE / THIS END MOVES A LOT

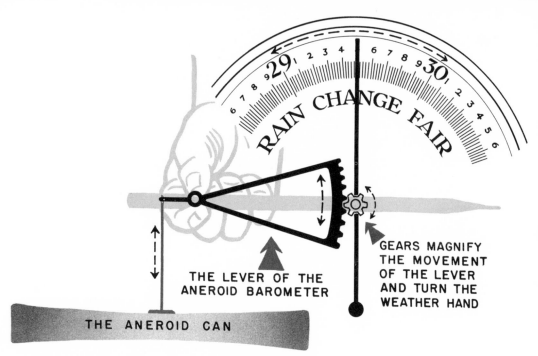

THE LEVER OF THE
ANEROID BAROMETER

GEARS MAGNIFY
THE MOVEMENT
OF THE LEVER
AND TURN THE
WEATHER HAND

THE ANEROID CAN

A lever like this could make the small motion of the can top big enough to see. In some aneroid barometers, the short end of such a lever is fastened to the center of the small tin can. The other end is connected to the hand on the dial.

When the air pressure changes, the can top bends or straightens only a little bit; then the hand moves far enough for you to see the change.

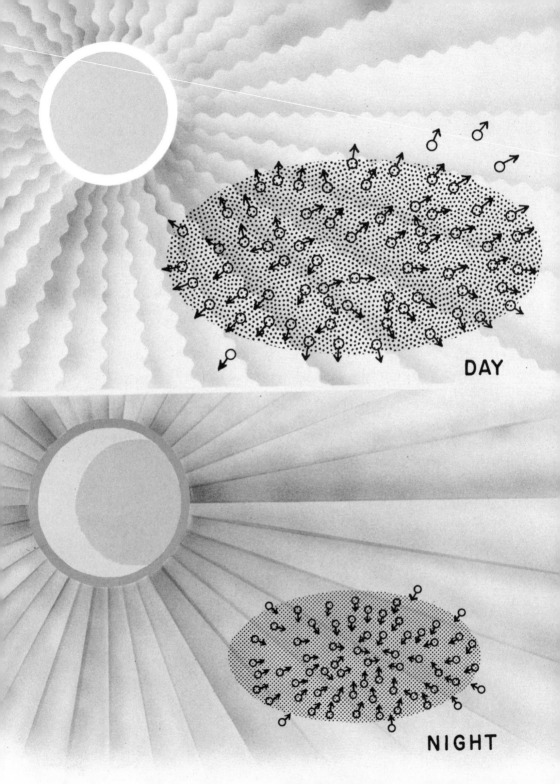

DAY

NIGHT

So both the mercury barometer and the aneroid barometer help the weatherman tell what the weather is going to be by measuring changes in air pressure.

But what makes air pressure change from day to day? Heat makes it change.

Heat comes to the earth from the sun, which is nearly one hundred million miles away. Air molecules take in the heat and it gives them energy to move. As they take in more energy, they move faster. To move faster they must go farther apart.

When this happens, there aren't as many molecules in the same spot as before. This means the air in that spot weighs less.

When night comes and there isn't any sunlight, the air molecules have no way to get energy. They lose some of their energy and cool off. When they cool off they slow down. They move closer together.

When air molecules slow down and move closer together, there are more of them in one spot. The air in that spot weighs more.

So heat makes air pressure change.

But another thing makes it change too.

Water makes it change.

When your mother hangs wet clothes on her clothesline, where does the water go as they dry?

It goes into the air.

Water is going into the air all the time—from lakes and oceans and streams. Sunlight warms the surface of the water. Some of the water molecules absorb the energy and move so fast they pop right up out of the lake or ocean. Then the water molecules move around in the air. This we call evaporation.

Each water molecule that goes into the air must have room to move about. To make room for itself, it pushes aside some air molecules.

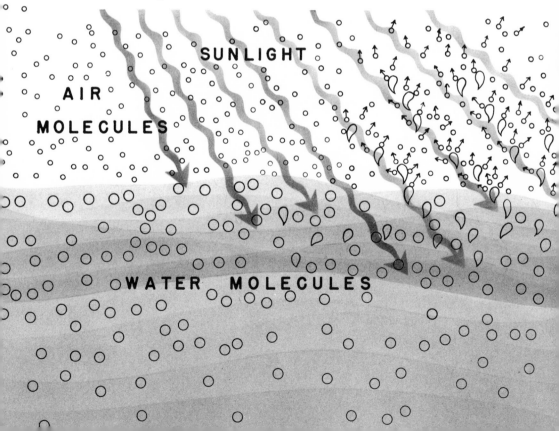

But water molecules are not as heavy as air molecules. Air mixed with water molecules is lighter than dry air.

When lots of water molecules are mixed with air molecules, the air feels damp. We call damp air "humid" air. When the summer air is very moist, people say "The humidity is high," and blame their discomfort on the high humidity. And it is true that humid air makes us feel uncomfortable.

Warm air can hold more water than cold air. If warm air with a lot of water molecules in it is cooled, the water comes out of it. First it forms clouds which are tiny droplets of water or ice. Then raindrops form and fall, or it begins to snow.

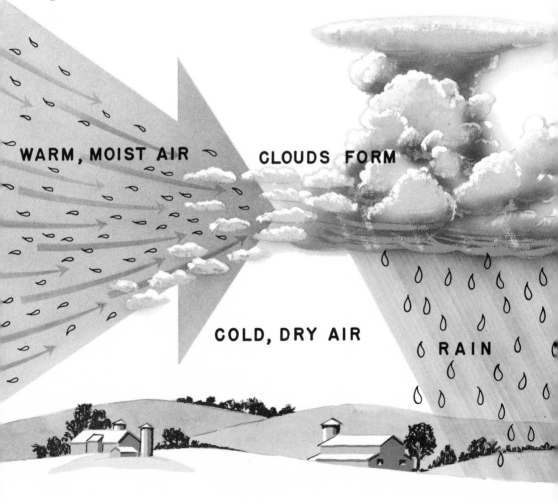

WARM, MOIST AIR   CLOUDS FORM

COLD, DRY AIR   RAIN

You can try an experiment to get water out of the air in your house. Take a glass and be sure it is dry on the outside. Put several ice cubes in it and fill it with water. Wait a minute or two, and then look carefully at the glass. Tiny droplets of water will be on the outside. On warm summer days, when the humidity is high, there will be a lot of tiny droplets on the glass. They may even run together into large drops that fall and make a puddle on the table.

U. S. 1502418

The water you see came from the air. As air passed near the cold glass, it was cooled. As the air cooled, water came out of it.

But when the air holds the water, that air is light. If it is warm, it is lighter still.

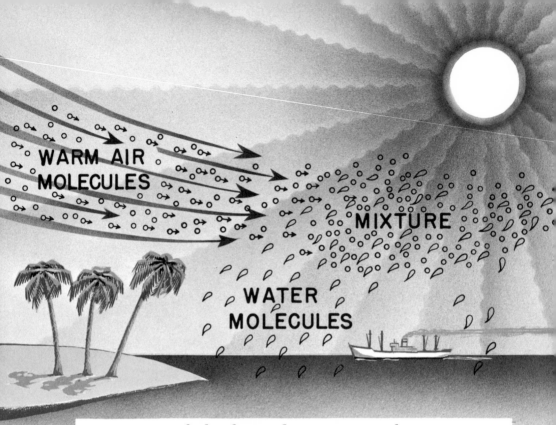

WARM AIR
MOLECULES

MIXTURE

WATER
MOLECULES

Most of the humid, warm air that comes to the United States is from near the equator. The sunlight is hottest near the equator because more of the sun's heat strikes the earth there than anywhere else. This heat warms the air. As the air moves and passes over the warm oceans, it mixes with water molecules that have evaporated.

Large amounts of this warm, humid air drift north and cover part of the United States.

Dry, cold air comes to the United States from far to the north, from Canada or the Arctic or from over the cold northern oceans. Large amounts of this cold, dry air drift south.

Where the warm, humid air and the cold, dry air meet, clouds form. Often there are storms with lots of rain. The air pressure changes rapidly. The barometer shows the weathermen all the changes.

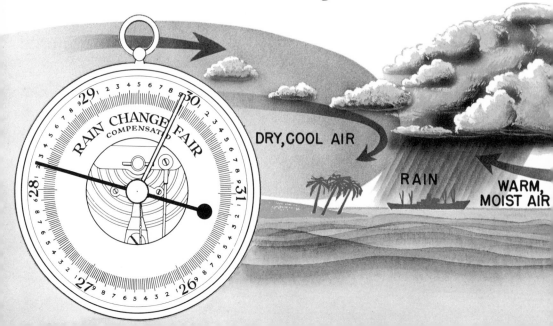

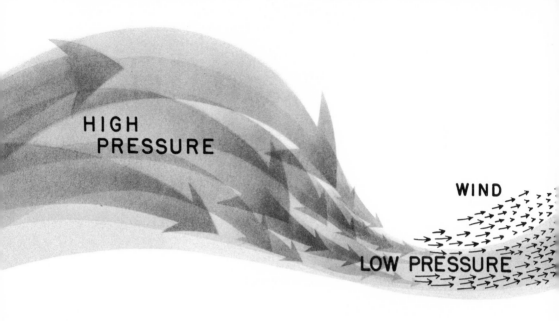

HIGH
PRESSURE

WIND

LOW PRESSURE

Cold, heavy air begins to flow toward the lighter air—just like water running downhill. In fact, you can think of heavy, cold, high-pressure air as a mountain and warm, humid, low-pressure air as a valley. The air flows from the mountain into the valley, and makes the wind.

Wind is millions of air molecules moving. They run into trees and bend the branches. They run into you, too, and you can feel the wind on your face.

Hurricanes are great circles of wind that come from near the equator. The air in the circle is *all* warm, and has a lot of water vapor in it; but it is warmest, and most humid, near the center. So the pressure there is lowest. Air flows inward to this center, forming a giant whirlpool of air—like water gurgling down a drain. But this whirlpool of air may be five hundred miles across!

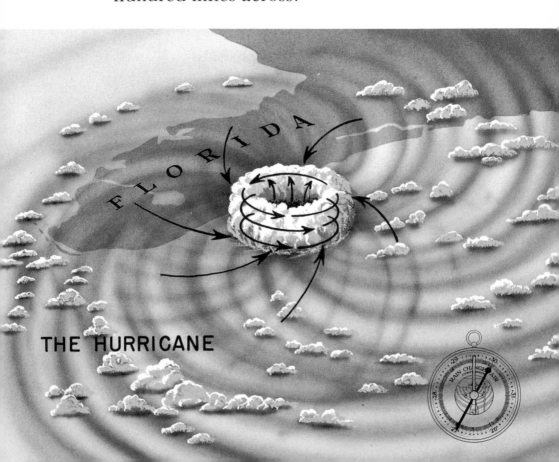

THE HURRICANE

The lower the pressure is in the center of the hurricane, the faster the wind blows. It can blow down trees and houses. It can wreck boats and blow the ocean far up onto the shore. Sometimes it blows faster than two hundred miles per hour!

Tornadoes are another kind of windstorm. They come from the meeting of great amounts of cold and warm air. The air mixes together, forming clouds, and great winds begin to blow.

Sometimes these winds form a small, but very strong, whirlpool of air. This whirlpool is filled with water vapor, which begins to condense. It hangs from a big cloud like a giant rope, reaching all the way to the earth. Where the whirlpool touches the earth, houses in its path are torn apart and trees are pulled up by their roots or snapped off.

Tornadoes are more fierce than hurricanes. Air moves around their whirlpools with a speed of five hundred miles per hour!

The barometer helps tell the weatherman when storms like these are coming. When the barometer is high, he doesn't worry. But when it starts to fall, he begins to watch it carefully. A storm may be on its way.

So the next time you hear a weather report, listen carefully. The weatherman may say something like this: *"The weather today will be fair and cool. Winds from the northwest at ten to fifteen miles per hour. The barometer reads thirty inches and is rising. . . ."*

You won't wonder then what a rising barometer is.

You'll know!

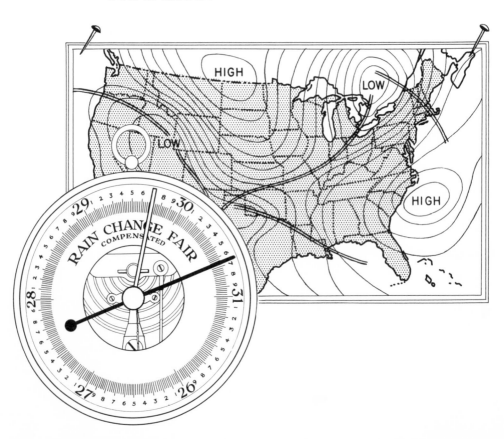